perfect cupcakes

FOG CITY PRESS

Published by Fog City Press
415 Jackson Street
San Francisco, CA 94111 USA

© 2008 Weldon Owen Inc.

Chief Executive Officer, Weldon Owen Group John Owen
Chief Executive Officer and President, Weldon Owen Inc. Terry Newell
Chief Financial Officer, Weldon Owen Group Simon Fraser
Vice President International Sales Stuart Laurence
Vice President and Creative Director Gaye Allen
Vice President and Publisher Roger Shaw
Managing Editor, Fog City Press Karen Perez
Editorial Assistant Sonia Vallabh
Project Editor Norman Kolpas
Project Designer Jason Budow
Senior Designer Kara Church
Designer, Revised Edition Andreas Schueller
New Photography Carin Krasner
New Recipe Development and Food Styling Karen Gillingham
Production Director Chris Hemesath
Sales Manager Emily Bartle
Color Manager Teri Bell
Production Manager Michelle Duggan

On the cover: Vanilla Sour Cream Cupcakes with Pink Frosting, recipe on
page 11; photo by Tucker + Hossler; food stylist Jen Straus; food stylist
assistant, Alexa Hyman.

ISBN-10: 1-74089-736-6
ISBN-13: 978-1-74089-736-5

First Printed 2008
10 9 8 7 6 5 4 3 2

Color separations by Embassy Graphics, Canada
Printed in China by SNP-Leefung Printers Ltd.

A Weldon Owen Production

perfect cupcakes

contents

introduction

What makes the perfect cupcake?

From the standpoint of baking, it starts with a great recipe and the right equipment. This collection of kitchen-tested recipes aims to provide reliably excellent results every time. All of them have been developed specifically to work with a six-cup muffin pan. You can choose a traditional metal pan, or a silicone muffin pan to safeguard against burning. You can spoon the batter into paper cupcake liners, or foil liners, or right into the pan.

These are the technicalities. But there's another way to approach the matter of cupcake perfection, and that is from the standpoint of taste. When it comes to personal taste, there is no one perfect cupcake apart from the kind that you think achieves perfection at any particular moment. That is why this collection organizes its 26 recipes by theme, to help you choose the right cupcake to suit any occasion or any mood. Each recipe also features an assortment of special, creative "Make It Different!" hints that will help you easily achieve many more variations, expanding the possibilities this little book offers to literally hundreds of different cupcakes.

After all, every day, indeed every moment, can have its own particular perfect cupcake.

cupcake basics

Great cupcakes are so easy to make that you don't really need much in the way of instructions beyond what you'll find in each of the recipes in this book. Nevertheless, being aware of a few guidelines will increase not only your success but also the pleasure you get from the process.

• **Read and follow the recipe.** Review the ingredients and instructions before starting. Do follow all instructions to the letter; don't take shortcuts, which could affect the results.

• **Use the right equipment.** All of the recipes in this book work with a six-cup muffin pan with standard ½-cup (125-ml) cups. If using a metal muffin pan, plan to grease the cups with nonstick baking spray, butter, or shortening, or to use paper cupcake or muffin liners. If using a flexible silicone tray, place it on a rigid metal baking sheet to hold it steady for filling and safe, easy transfer into and out of the oven.

• **Prep ingredients in advance and measure precisely.** Before you start preparing any recipe, follow its ingredients list for specifics on how to measure and prepare each item. Have all the prepped ingredients lined up in your work area, ready to use at the right moment.

• **Have fun**. Try the recipe variations. Visit gourmet shops for pretty decorations like edible sugar flowers to make your own original creations. After all, that's what cupcakes are all about!

chocolate chip
cupcakes

Think of these as chocolate chip cookies in cupcake form, plus dollops of chocolate frosting.

● Preheat the oven to 350°F (180°C). Prepare a 6-cup standard (½-cup/125-ml) muffin pan by greasing or inserting liners.

● In a medium bowl, whisk together the flour and sugar, then add the chocolate chips. In a small mixing bowl, combine the egg, milk, melted butter, and vanilla. Add to the flour mixture and stir until just moistened. Divide among the prepared cups.

● Bake until the tops spring back when lightly tapped, 20–25 minutes. Remove from the oven and cool in the pan for 10 minutes, then transfer to a wire rack to cool.

● For the frosting, put the chocolate, cream, and butter in a heatproof bowl over but not touching a pan of simmering water. Stir gently over low heat until smooth. Chill until firm but spreadable, then pipe or spread over the cooled cupcakes.

Make It Different!

● *Use white chocolate chips instead of the semisweet (plain) and milk chocolate ones.*

● *Add a few tablespoons of roasted peanuts, pecans, or walnuts to the batter.*

● *Top the cupcakes with white chocolate frosting or Vanilla Buttercream (page 15).*

makes 6

cupcakes

1 cup (5 oz/155 g)
self-rising flour

¼ cup (2 oz/60 g) sugar

¼ cup (1⅓ oz/40 g) each
semisweet (plain) and milk
chocolate chips

1 egg, lightly beaten

½ cup (4 fl oz/125 ml) milk

3 tablespoons (1½ oz/45 g)
butter, melted

½ teaspoon vanilla extract
(essence)

chocolate frosting

1½ oz (45 g) semisweet
(plain) chocolate, chopped

2 tablespoons heavy
(double) cream

¾ tablespoon butter

makes 6

1 cup (4 oz/125 g) cake
(soft-wheat) flour

1 teaspoon baking powder

¼ teaspoon salt

¼ cup (2 oz/60 g) unsalted
butter, at room temperature

½ cup (4 oz/125 g) sugar

1 egg

½ teaspoon vanilla extract
(essence)

⅓ cup (3 fl oz/90 ml) sour
cream

Vanilla Buttercream
(page 15)

Red food coloring

6 hard candy flowers, for
decoration

vanilla sour cream
cupcakes

Look in baking supplies or gourmet food shops for candy flowers to top these pretty cupcakes.

• Preheat the oven to 350°F (180°C). Prepare a 6-cup standard (½-cup/125-ml) muffin pan by greasing or inserting liners.

• In a small bowl, whisk together the flour, baking powder, and salt. In a medium bowl, using a hand-held mixer on medium speed, beat together the butter and sugar until light. Beat in the egg and vanilla until well blended. Gradually beat half of the dry ingredients into the butter mixture, then half of the sour cream; repeat with the remaining dry ingredients and sour cream.

• Divide the batter evenly among the prepared muffin cups. Bake until the tops spring back when lightly tapped, 20–25 minutes.

• Cool on a wire rack for 10 minutes, then turn out the cupcakes and cool completely on the rack. Meanwhile, make the buttercream, beating in just

a few drops of the red food coloring to achieve the desired pink color. Spoon this frosting into a piping bag fitted with a large star tip and, starting near each cupcake's edge, pipe it in a spiral to form a mound on top of the cupcake. Top the frosting with a hard candy flower.

Make It Different!

• *Substitute Chocolate Frosting (page 8) or any other frosting you like for the buttercream.*

• *Try a different flavoring extract (essence) in place of vanilla.*

• *In place of the candy flowers, decorate with crystallized violet or rose petals, or popular candies like jelly beans.*

peanut butter
& banana cupcakes

One of the all-time popular flavor combinations comes together in these deliciously gooey cupcakes.

● Preheat the oven to 350°F (180°C). Prepare a 6-cup standard (½-cup/125-ml) muffin pan by greasing or inserting liners.

● In a small bowl, whisk together the flour, baking powder, and salt. In a medium bowl, using a hand-held mixer on medium speed, beat together the sugar and peanut butter until light. Beat in the egg, then the mashed banana. Gradually beat in the dry ingredients just until combined. Divide the batter equally among the prepared cups.

● Bake until the tops spring back when lightly tapped, 20–25 minutes. Cool on a wire rack for 5 minutes, then turn out and cool completely.

● Meanwhile, melt the butter in a skillet over medium heat. Add the banana slices and sauté until browned, about 1 minute; turn them over and brown on the other side. Transfer to paper towels to cool.

● For the frosting, put the peanut butter in a small bowl and use a hand-held mixer on medium speed to beat until fluffy. Gradually beat in the sugar. Beat in enough of the cream to reach a spreading consistency. Stir in the peanuts.

● Spread the frosting on the cooled cupcakes. Top with banana slices.

Make It Different!

● *Substitute almond butter, cashew butter, or hazelnut (filbert) butter for the peanut butter.*

● *Cut the cupcakes horizontally in half and add a layer of Chocolate Frosting (page 8).*

● *Spoon a dollop of jelly in the middle of the batter in each cup, or on top of the frosting.*

makes 6

cupcakes

1 cup (4 oz/125 g) cake
(soft-wheat) flour

1 teaspoon baking powder

¼ teaspoon salt

½ cup (4 oz/125 g) sugar

¼ cup (2 oz/60 g) creamy
peanut butter

1 egg

½ cup (4 oz/125 g) mashed
ripe banana (1 small
banana)

1 tablespoon butter

1 banana, sliced

chunky peanut butter
frosting

¾ cup (6 oz/185 g) creamy
peanut butter

½ cup (2½ oz/75 g)
confectioners' (icing) sugar

1–2 tablespoons heavy
(double) cream

¼ cup (1 oz/30 g) coarsely
chopped roasted peanuts

makes 6

cupcakes

¾ cup (3 oz/90 g) cake
(soft-wheat) flour

1 teaspoon baking powder

¼ teaspoon salt

¼ cup (2 oz/60 g) unsalted
butter, at room temperature

¼ cup (2 oz/60 g) sugar

1 egg

½ teaspoon vanilla extract
(essence)

⅓ cup (3 oz/85 ml) milk

¼ cup (1 oz/30 g) multi-
colored confetti sprinkles

vanilla buttercream

1½ cups (8 oz/240 g)
confectioners' (icing) sugar

½ cup (4 oz/125 g)
unsalted butter, at room
temperature

½ teaspoon vanilla extract
(essence)

1–2 tablespoons heavy
(double) cream

vanilla rainbow
cupcakes

Mixed into the batter, a scattering of colorful confetti sprinkles makes these cupcakes extra festive.

● Preheat the oven to 350°F (180°C). Prepare a 6-cup standard (½-cup/125-ml) muffin pan by greasing or inserting liners.

● In a small bowl, whisk together the cake flour, baking powder, and salt. In a medium bowl, using a hand-held electric mixer on medium speed, cream together the butter and sugar until well blended. Beat in the egg and vanilla until light. Gradually beat in half of the flour mixture. Beat in the milk and then the remaining flour mixture until blended. Fold in half of the sprinkles. Divide the batter equally among the prepared cups.

● Bake until the tops spring back when lightly tapped, 20–25 minutes. Cool on a wire rack for 10 minutes, then turn out and cool completely.

● Meanwhile, make the Vanilla Buttercream. In a medium bowl, use a hand-held mixer on medium speed to beat together the confectioners' sugar and butter until blended. Beat in the vanilla; then, beat in enough of the cream to achieve a soft consistency suitable for spreading or piping.

● Fill a pastry bag fitted with the large star tip with the Vanilla Buttercream and pipe it onto the cupcakes. Scatter the remaining sprinkles over the frosting.

Make It Different!

● *Replace the confetti sprinkles with rainbow sprinkles (jimmies) in both the batter and on top.*

● *Substitute Chocolate Frosting (page 8) for the Vanilla Buttercream.*

● *Instead of sprinkles on top, use shiny edible silver or gold dragees.*

15

poundcake cupcakes
with lemon-lime glaze

Dense, moist, and delicious, these treats gain extra flavor from a sweet citrus-flavored topping.

- Preheat the oven to 350°F (180°C).

- In a small bowl, whisk together the cake flour, baking powder, and salt. In a separate bowl, beat the eggs together with the sour cream and vanilla. In a large mixing bowl, using a hand-held mixer on medium speed, cream together the butter and sugar until well blended. Beat in about a third of the egg mixture, then half of the dry ingredients; then another third of the eggs, then the remaining dry ingredients; and finally the remaining egg mixture until completely blended.

- Divide the batter equally among 6 standard (½-cup/125-ml) greased or lined muffin cups.

- Bake until the tops spring back when lightly tapped, 20–25 minutes. Cool on a wire rack for 5 minutes.

- Meanwhile, in a small bowl, stir together the confectioners' (icing) sugar and lemon and lime juices and zests.

- Turn out the cupcakes, place the wire rack over a sheet of waxed paper, and return them to the rack. Spoon citrus glaze generously over the warm cupcakes, allowing some to run down the sides. Serve warm or cooled.

> **Make It Different!**
>
> - *Add 1 tablespoon of grated citrus zest to the cupcake batter.*
>
> - *Substitute orange or mandarin juice and zest for some or all of the lemon or lime.*
>
> - *Garnish the tops with thin strips of citrus zest or candied peel.*

makes 6

1½ cups (6 oz/185 g) cake (soft-wheat) flour

1 teaspoon baking powder

¼ teaspoon salt

3 eggs

2 tablespoons sour cream

1 teaspoon vanilla extract (essence)

¾ cup (6 oz/185 g) unsalted butter, at room temperature

¼ cup (2 oz/60 g) sugar

1 cup (5 oz/155 g) confectioners' (icing) sugar

1½ teaspoons each freshly squeezed lemon and lime juice

1 teaspoon each grated lemon and lime zest

makes 6

½ cup (4 oz/125 g) sugar

½ cup (4 oz/125 g) butter, chopped into small pieces

¾ teaspoon vanilla extract (essence)

2 eggs

1⅓ cups (7 oz/215 g) self-rising flour, sifted

¼ teaspoon baking soda (bicarbonate of soda)

¾ cup (6 fl oz/180 ml) sour cream

⅔ cup (3⅓ oz/100 g) chopped pecans

½ teaspoon ground cinnamon

1 tablespoon plus 1 teaspoon firmly packed light brown sugar

pecan coffeecake
cupcakes

An excuse for eating cupcakes in the morning, these get a velvety texture from sour cream in the batter.

- Preheat the oven to 350°F (180°C).

- In a food processor with the stainless-steel blade, combine the sugar, butter, vanilla, eggs, flour, baking soda, and sour cream. Process until smooth, 1–2 minutes.

- Distribute half of the batter evenly among the cups of a 6-cup standard (½-cup/125-ml) greased or paper-lined muffin pan.

- In a small bowl, combine the pecans, cinnamon, and brown sugar. Sprinkle half over the batter in the pan. Top with the remaining batter, then sprinkle with the remaining pecan mixture.

- Bake until the cupcakes spring back when lightly touched, 20–25 minutes. Cool in the pan for 5 minutes. Serve warm, or transfer to a wire rack to cool.

Make It Different!

- *Replace the pecans with walnuts or hazelnuts (filberts).*

- *Try crème fraîche, French-style cultured cream, in place of the sour cream.*

- *Drizzle the warm cupcakes with a simple glaze made by stirring together 1 cup (5 oz/150 g) confectioners' (icing) sugar and 1–2 tablespoons milk.*

orange zest
cupcakes

Shredded orange zest and a dusting of sugar adorn these light and airy cupcakes.

- Preheat the oven to 350°F (180°C). Prepare a 6-cup standard (½-cup/125-ml) muffin pan by greasing or inserting liners.

- For the topping, in a small bowl, combine 1 teaspoon of the sugar and ½ teaspoon of the orange zest, pressing the zest into the sugar with the back of a spoon. Set aside.

- In a mixing bowl, stir together the flour, baking powder, salt, and remaining orange zest. Stir in the remaining sugar. In a small mixing bowl, combine the egg, milk, melted butter, and orange juice concentrate. Add all at once to the flour mixture and stir just until moistened.

- Divide the batter equally among the prepared cups. Sprinkle the tops with the sugar-orange mixture. Bake until the tops spring back when lightly tapped, 20–25 minutes. Cool on a wire rack for 10 minutes, then turn out and cool completely.

Make It Different!

- *Add 1 teaspoon ground ginger to the dry ingredients for the batter.*

- *Spoon a dollop of orange marmalade into the center of the batter in each cup.*

- *Top each cupcake with Chocolate Frosting (page 8), which tastes great with orange.*

makes 6

¼ cup (2 oz/60 g) plus
1 teaspoon sugar

1½ teaspoons finely
shredded orange zest

¾ cup (3 oz/90 g) cake (soft
wheat) flour

¾ teaspoon baking powder

Pinch of salt

1 egg, beaten

¼ cup (2 fl oz/60 ml) milk

2 tablespoons melted butter

1 tablespoon frozen orange
juice concentrate, thawed

makes 6

¼ cup (2 oz/60 g) butter

¼ cup (2 fl oz/60 ml) light molasses (golden syrup)

¾ cup (3½ oz/105 g) self-rising flour

⅜ cup (2¼ oz/65 g) whole wheat (wholemeal) flour

1 tablespoon ground ginger

¼ teaspoon baking soda (bicarbonate of soda)

3 tablespoons firmly packed light brown sugar

1 egg, lightly beaten

½ cup (4 fl oz/125 ml) milk

2 tablespoons candied (glacé) ginger, chopped, plus more for garnish

1 small ripe pear, peeled, cored, and chopped

½ cup (2½ oz/75 g) confectioners' (icing) sugar, sifted

gingerbread pear
cupcakes

An old-time favorite cake translates well into cupcakes, especially with the addition of sweet, juicy pear.

• Preheat the oven to 350°F (180°C). Prepare a 6-cup standard (½-cup/125-ml) muffin pan by greasing or inserting liners.

• In a small saucepan over low heat, gently melt half of the butter with all but ½ teaspoon of the molasses. Stir to combine, then set aside to cool.

• In a large mixing bowl, sift together the flours, ¾ tablespoon ground ginger, and baking soda, returning the husks to the bowl. Stir in the brown sugar. In a small mixing bowl, combine the egg, milk, and cooled butter and molasses mixture. Add all at once to the flour mixture along with the candied ginger and chopped pear. Stir just until moistened. Divide among the prepared cups.

• Bake until the tops spring back when lightly tapped, 20–25 minutes. Cool on a wire rack for 5 minutes, then turn out and cool completely.

• In a small saucepan over low heat, melt the remaining butter and molasses. Add the confectioners' icing sugar and remaining ground ginger and stir until melted and smooth. Spread immediately over the cupcakes and garnish with more candied ginger.

Make It Different!

• *Try chopped apple in place of the pear.*

• *Add a tiny dash of grated nutmeg to the dry ingredients with the ground ginger.*

• *Serve the cupcakes warm with vanilla ice cream instead of the frosting.*

double-decker
carrot cupcakes

Wholesome and delicious, these easy cupcakes have an extra layer of luscious frosting spread just underneath their crowns.

● Preheat the oven to 350°F (180°C).

● In a medium mixing bowl, whisk together the flour, baking powder, salt, and spices. In a separate bowl, using a hand-held electric mixer on medium speed, beat together the eggs, sugars, and oil. Stir into the dry ingredients just until blended. Stir in the carrot and chopped walnuts.

● Divide the batter equally among 6-cup standard (½-cup/125-ml) greased or paper-lined muffin pan. Bake until the tops spring back when tapped lightly, 20–25 minutes. Cool on a wire rack for 5 minutes, then turn out the cupcakes and cool completely.

● Meanwhile, make the Cream Cheese Frosting. In a mixing bowl, use a hand-held mixer on medium speed to beat together the butter, cream cheese, sugar, and vanilla until smooth.

● With a serrated knife, cut each cupcake in half horizontally. Spread some of the Cream Cheese Frosting over the cut surface of the bottom halves. Replace the top halves, and frost them generously.

Make It Different!

● *Substitute chopped pecans for the walnuts.*

● *Add a few drops of orange food coloring to the frosting.*

● *Top each cupcake with a roasted or candied walnut half.*

makes 6

cupcakes

1 cup (5 oz/155 g)
all-purpose (plain) flour

1 teaspoon baking powder

¼ teaspoon salt

1 teaspoon ground
cinnamon

¼ teaspoon grated nutmeg

2 eggs

½ cup (3 oz/90 g) firmly
packed light brown sugar

½ cup (4 oz/125 g) sugar

½ cup (125 ml) vegetable oil

1½ cups (7 oz/215 g)
grated carrot

½ cup (2 oz/60 g) chopped
walnuts

cream cheese frosting

¼ cup (2 oz/60 g) butter,
at room temperature

4 ounces (125 g)
cream cheese, at room
temperature

1 cup (5 oz/155 g)
confectioners' (icing) sugar

½ teaspoon vanilla extract
(essence)

makes 6

2½ oz (75 g) butter

1 cup (5 oz/155 g)
self-rising flour

⅔ cup (2 oz/60 g) grated
dried (dessicated) coconut

⅓ cup (3 oz/90 g) sugar

1 egg, lightly beaten

½ cup (4 fl oz/125 ml) milk

1 teaspoon grated
lemon zest

2 tablespoons lemon juice

¼ cup (1¼ oz/35 g)
all-purpose (plain) flour

Vanilla Buttercream
(page 15)

⅔ cup (2 oz/60 g)
sweetened shredded
coconut

lemon coconut
cupcakes

The richness of coconut and the zesty taste of lemon are natural partners in these festive cupcakes.

● Preheat the oven to 350°F (180°C). Prepare a 6-cup standard (½-cup/125-ml) muffin pan by greasing or inserting liners. Melt 1½ tablespoons of the butter; put the remainder in the refrigerator to chill.

● In a large mixing bowl, sift the self-rising flour. Stir in ½ cup (1½ oz/45 g) of the grated coconut and ¼ cup (2 oz/60 g) of the sugar. Make a well in the center. In a small bowl, combine the egg, milk, melted butter, zest, and juice. Add all at once to the flour mixture and stir just until moistened. Divide evenly among the prepared cups.

● Put the all-purpose flour and remaining grated coconut and sugar in a small bowl. Cut the chilled butter into cubes and rub it into the dry ingredients with your fingertips until the mixture resembles coarse crumbs. Spoon evenly over the cupcakes.

● Bake until the tops are springy when lightly tapped, 20–25 minutes. Cool in the pan for 5 minutes, then turn out to cool completely. Spread the Vanilla Buttercream on top and sprinkle evenly with the coconut shreds, pressing them gently into the buttercream.

Make It Different!

● *For an even more intense coconut flavor, use the thick layer of cream from the top of a can of coconut milk in place of the melted butter in the batter.*

● *Use orange zest and juice in place of the lemon.*

● *Top the icing with strips of candied (glacé) lemon peel.*

black & white
cupcakes

A favorite deli-style cookie translates perfectly into cupcakes topped with two different icings.

● Preheat the oven to 350°F (180°C). Prepare a 6-cup standard (½-cup/125-ml) muffin pan by greasing or inserting liners.

● In a medium bowl, whisk together the sugar, sour cream, oil, egg, and vanilla. Sift in the flour, cocoa, and baking soda. Stir until blended. Divide the batter equally among the prepared cups.

● Bake until the tops spring back when lightly tapped, 20–25 minutes. Cool on a wire rack for 10 minutes, then turn out to cool completely.

● Meanwhile, make the icings. For the Chocolate Icing, combine the cream and corn syrup in a small, heavy saucepan and bring to a simmer over medium-low heat. Remove from the heat and stir in the chocolate chips until smooth. Let cool until it reaches a thick but fluid spreading consistency.

For the White Icing, in a small bowl, stir together the sugar, vanilla, and enough of the cream to form a smooth icing.

● Spread each icing over half of the top of each cupcake. Let stand until set, about 1 hour.

Make It Different!

● *Use white chocolate chips in place of the semisweet in the Chocolate Icing.*

● *Color the White Icing with a few drops of food coloring.*

● *Scatter white chocolate chips over the brown icing and dark chocolate chips over the white icing.*

makes 6

cupcakes

½ cup (4 oz/125 g) sugar

½ cup (4 fl oz/125 ml) sour cream

⅓ cup (3 fl oz/90 ml) vegetable oil

1 egg

½ teaspoon vanilla extract (essence)

¾ cup (3 oz/90 g) cake (soft-wheat) flour

⅓ cup (1¼ oz/40 g) unsweetened cocoa powder

¾ teaspoon baking soda (bircarbonate of soda)

chocolate icing

2 tablespoons heavy (double) cream

2 teaspoons light corn syrup

⅓ cup (1⅔ oz/50 g) semisweet (plain) mini chocolate chips

white icing

½ cup (2½ oz/75 g) confectioners' (icing) sugar

¼ teaspoon vanilla extract (essence)

1–2 tablespoons heavy (double) cream

makes 6

1 cup (5 oz/155 g) self-
rising flour

¼ teaspoon baking soda
(bicarbonate of soda)

3 tablespoons unsweetened
cocoa powder

¼ cup (2 oz/60 g) sugar

¼ cup (1¾ oz/50 g) milk
chocolate chips

½ cup (2¾ oz/80 g)
semisweet (plain) chocolate
chips

1 egg, lightly beaten

¾ cup (6 fl oz/180 ml) milk

2 tablespoons butter,
melted

triple-chocolate
cupcakes

Three different sources of rich chocolate flavor make these easy cupcakes three times as delicious for chocolate lovers.

● Preheat the oven to 350°F (180°C). Prepare a 6-cup standard (½-cup/125-ml) muffin pan by greasing or inserting liners.

● In a mixing bowl, whisk together the flour, baking soda, and cocoa. Stir in the sugar, all of the milk chocolate chips, and half of the semisweet (plain) chips. In a small bowl, mix the egg, milk, and butter. Add all at once to the flour mixture and stir until just moistened.

● Divide the batter evenly among the prepared cups. Bake until the tops spring back when lightly touched, 20–25 minutes. Cool in the pan for 5 minutes, then turn out onto a wire rack to cool completely.

● Meanwhile, put the remaining chocolate chips in a microwave-safe bowl and melt in short bursts in the microwave. Stir until smooth. Using a teaspoon, swirl the melted chocolate thickly over the top of each cupcake.

Make It Different!

● *Substitute white chocolate chips for some or all of the milk chocolate chips in the batter.*

● *Use white chocolate instead of semisweet chips for the melted chocolate icing.*

● *While the melted chocolate icing is still soft, decorate it with sprinkles (jimmies).*

chocolate cherry
cupcakes

Whether fresh, bottled, or canned, cherries show their special affinity for chocolate in these cupcakes.

● Preheat the oven to 350°F (180°C). Prepare a 6-cup standard (½-cup/125-ml) muffin pan by greasing or inserting liners.

● In a mixing bowl, whisk together the flour and allspice. Stir in the almonds, sugar, chocolate chips, and cherries. In a small mixing bowl, combine the egg, butter, and buttermilk. Add all at once to the flour mixture and stir just until moistened. Divide the batter evenly among the prepared cups.

● Bake until the tops spring back when lightly tapped, 20–25 minutes. Cool on a wire rack for 5 minutes, then turn out and cool completely.

Make It Different!

● *In the early summer season, look for beautiful fresh gold-and-red Rainier cherries to use in the batter.*

● *Replace the ground almonds in the batter with ground hazelnuts (filberts).*

● *Spread the cupcakes with Chocolate Frosting (page 8).*

makes 6

1 cup (5 oz/105 g) self-rising flour

½ teaspoon ground allspice

2 tablespoons ground almonds

2½ tablespoons firmly packed light brown sugar

½ cup (2¾ oz/80 g) semisweet (plain) chocolate chips

½ cup (3 oz/90 g) bottled or canned sweet red cherries, pitted and drained, or same quantity fresh sweet cherries, pitted

1 egg, lightly beaten

3 tablespoons butter, melted

⅓ cup (3 fl oz/90 ml) buttermilk

makes 6

1 (20-ounce/600-g) can
pineapple tidbits

¼ cup (1½ oz/45 g) packed
light brown sugar

½ cup (4 oz/125 g)
unsalted butter, melted

1 cup (4 oz/125 g) cake
(soft-wheat) flour

½ teaspoon baking powder

¼ teaspoon salt

2 egg yolks

⅓ cup (3 oz/90 g) sugar

Softly whipped cream,
optional

6 maraschino cherries
with stems

pineapple upside-down
cupcakes

A favorite old-fashioned novelty cake becomes an exciting new treat when you prepare it in the form of individual cupcakes.

• Preheat the oven to 350°F (180°C).

• Drain the pineapple, reserving ½ cup (4¼ fl oz/ 125 ml) of its juice. In the bottom of each cup of a 6-cup standard (½-cup/125-ml) silicone muffin pan or a greased metal muffin pan, neatly arrange 7 pineapple pieces in a circle. (Reserve any leftover pineapple pieces for another use.) Sprinkle each arrangement with 2 teaspoons brown sugar. Drizzle 2 teaspoons melted butter into each cup. Set aside.

• In a small bowl, whisk together the flour, baking powder, and salt. In a separate bowl, using a hand-held electric mixer on medium speed, beat together the egg yolks, sugar, and remaining butter until light. Gradually beat in half of the dry ingredients. Beat in the reserved pineapple juice, then the remaining dry ingredients until well blended. Spoon the batter evenly into the prepared cups. Bake until the centers spring back when touched

lightly, 20–25 minutes. Cool in the pan on a wire rack for 10 minutes. Then, carefully invert onto a baking sheet or tray to unmold, rearranging any pineapple bits as necessary. Transfer with a spatula to individual serving dishes and serve warm or at room temperature, garnishing each with a dollop of whipped cream and a cherry.

Make It Different!

• *Add 2 tablespoons chopped macadamia nuts to the batter.*

• *Substitute other canned fruit in syrup such as apricots, pitted cherries, or peaches.*

• *Sprinkle sweetened coconut shreds over the pineapple before adding the batter.*

red-hot red velvet
cupcakes

Cocoa powder, cinnamon candies, and red food coloring give these cupcakes devilish flavor and color.

- Preheat the oven to 350°F (180°C). Prepare a 6-cup standard (½-cup/125-ml) muffin pan by greasing or inserting liners.

- In a medium bowl, whisk together the flour, sugar, cocoa powder, 2 teaspoons of the crushed candies, the baking soda, and salt. Set aside. In a medium bowl, using a hand-held mixer on medium speed, lightly beat the egg. Beat in the buttermilk, vinegar, oil, food coloring, and vanilla. Beat in the dry ingredients until thoroughly blended. Divide the batter equally among the prepared cups.

- Bake until the tops spring back when lightly tapped, 20–25 minutes. Cool on a wire rack for 10 minutes, then turn out and cool completely.

- Place the frosting in a pastry bag fitted with the large plain tip. Pipe dollops of frosting onto the cupcakes. Sprinkle with the remaining crushed candies.

Make It Different!

- *Use ground cinnamon in place of the crushed candies in the batter.*

- *Substitute Vanilla Buttercream (page 15) or Chocolate Frosting (page 8) for the Cream Cheese Frosting.*

- *Decorate the cupcakes with red-hot cinnamon-flavored jellybeans.*

makes 6

¾ cup (3¾ oz/115 g) unbleached all-purpose (plain) flour

½ cup (4 oz/125 g) sugar

¼ cup (1¼ oz/35 g) unsweetened cocoa powder

1 small box (1 oz/30 g) hot cinnamon-flavored candies, crushed

½ teaspoon baking soda (bicarbonate of soda)

½ teaspoon salt

1 egg

⅓ cup (3 fl oz/90 ml) buttermilk

½ teaspoon distilled white vinegar

⅓ cup (3 fl oz/90 ml) vegetable oil

5 teaspoons red food coloring

½ teaspoon vanilla extract (essence)

Cream Cheese Frosting (page 24)

makes 6

mexican streusel topping

3 tablespoons almond meal

3 tablespoons all-purpose (plain) flour

1 tablespoon packed light brown sugar

2 tablespoons unsalted butter, chilled

½ disk (about 1½ oz/45 g) Mexican chocolate, roughly chopped

cupcakes

½ cup (3 oz/90 g) almond meal

½ cup (2 oz/60 g) cake (soft-wheat) flour

½ teaspoon baking soda (bicarbonate of soda)

¼ teaspoon salt

¼ cup (2 oz/60 g) unsalted butter

1 disk (about 3 oz/90 g) Mexican chocolate, finely chopped

2 eggs, separated

¼ cup (2 oz/60 g) sugar

¼ cup (2 fl oz/60 ml) sour cream

mexican chocolate streusel cupcakes

Look for exotic cinnamon-spiced Mexican chocolate in the ethnic foods aisle, Latino markets, or online.

- First, prepare the topping. In a small bowl, combine the almond meal, flour, and brown sugar. Rub the butter into the mixture until it resembles coarse meal. Stir in the chocolate. Refrigerate.

- Preheat the oven to 350°F (180°C). Prepare a 6-cup standard (½-cup/125-ml) muffin pan by greasing or inserting liners.

- For the cupcakes, in a small bowl, whisk together the almond meal, flour, baking soda, and salt. In a saucepan, melt the butter over low heat. Stir in the chocolate until smooth. Set aside.

- In a medium bowl, using a hand-held electric mixer on medium speed, beat the egg yolks and sugar together until thick and pale yellow. Gradually beat in the cooled chocolate mixture. Gradually beat in half of the dry ingredients, then the sour cream, and then the remaining dry ingredients.

- Beat the egg whites until they hold stiff peaks. With a rubber spatula, gently fold about a third of the whites into the batter. Then, in two more batches, fold in the remaining whites, blending completely.

- Divide the batter among the prepared muffin cups. Crumble the streusel on top. Bake until the tops spring back when lightly tapped, 25–30 minutes. Cool on a wire rack for 5 minutes, then turn out and cool completely. Serve warm or cooled.

> ### Make It Different!
>
> - *Add 1 teaspoon of instant espresso coffee granules to the yolk mixture.*
>
> - *Include a tiny pinch of pure red chile powder for an intriguing hint of heat.*
>
> - *Look for piloncillo, robust-tasting unrefined Mexican brown sugar, to use in the streusel.*

white chocolate raspberry cupcakes

The tang of raspberries counterpoints white chocolate's creamy richness in these decadent treats.

● Preheat the oven to 350°F (180°C). Prepare a 6-cup standard (½-cup/125-ml) muffin pan by greasing or inserting liners.

● In a small saucepan over low heat, melt half the white chocolate chips with the butter, stirring gently until smooth. Set aside to cool.

● In a mixing bowl, sift the flour. Stir in the sugar and remaining white chocolate chips. In a small mixing bowl, combine the egg, milk, and the melted butter and chocolate mixture. Add all at once to the flour mixture together with the raspberries. Stir until just moistened. Divide the batter evenly among the prepared cups.

● Bake until the tops spring back when lightly tapped, 20–25 minutes. Cool on a wire rack for 5 minutes, then turn out. Serve warm, dusted with sifted confectioners' (icing) sugar.

Make It Different!

● *Substitute milk or semisweet (plain) chocolate chips for the whole white chocolate chips stirred into the batter.*

● *Add 1 teaspoon vanilla or almond extract (essence) to the batter.*

● *Top the cupcakes with Chocolate Frosting (page 8), substituting white chocolate for the regular chocolate.*

makes 6

½ cup (3 oz/90 g) white chocolate chips

2 tablespoons butter

1 cup (5 oz/155 g) self-rising flour

¼ cup (2 oz/60 g) sugar

1 egg, lightly beaten

½ cup (4 fl oz/125 ml) milk

¾ cup (3 oz/90 g) fresh or frozen raspberries

Confectioners' (icing) sugar, for dusting

makes 6

½ cup (3 oz/90 g) chopped dates

⅔ cup (3¾ oz/115 g) firmly packed light brown sugar

⅓ cup (3 oz/90 g) butter

5 fl oz (150 ml) water

½ teaspoon baking soda (bicarbonate of soda)

½ teaspoon vanilla extract (essence)

¾ cup (3½ oz/105 g) self-rising flour

¼ cup (1½ oz/45 g) whole wheat (wholemeal) flour

¼ cup (1 oz/30 g) chopped pecans

1 egg, lightly beaten

¼ cup (2 fl oz/60 ml) heavy (double) cream

warm date-nut cupcakes
with caramel sauce

Served still warm from the oven and dripping with their easily prepared rich sauce, these cupcakes taste absolutely decadent.

• Preheat the oven to 350°F (180°C).

• Put the dates, half of the brown sugar, ¼ cup (2 oz/60 g) of butter, and water in a medium saucepan. Stir over low heat until the butter has melted. Still over low heat, bring to a boil and boil for 2 minutes. Remove from the heat, cool slightly, then stir in the baking soda and vanilla. Set aside.

• In a large mixing bowl, sift together the flours. Stir in the pecans. Add the beaten egg to the date mixture. Add all at once to the flour mixture and stir just until moistened. Divide equally among the cups of a 6-cup standard (½-cup/125-ml) greased or paper-lined muffin pan. Bake until the tops spring back when lightly tapped, 20–25 minutes.

• Meanwhile, put the remaining brown sugar and butter and the cream in a small saucepan. Stir over low heat until the sugar has dissolved. Bring to a low boil and boil for 1 minute. Let the cupcakes cool in the pan for 5 minutes, then brush with a little of the caramel sauce. Remove from the pan and serve warm with the remaining hot caramel sauce.

> ### Make It Different!
>
> • *Substitute chopped walnuts for the pecans.*
>
> • *Stir a little grated lime zest into the warm caramel sauce.*
>
> • *After spooning on the remaining caramel sauce, add a dollop of whipped cream to each serving.*

passion fruit
cupcakes

Sweet and tangy passion fruit gives both the batter and the icing of these simple cupcakes an exotic tropical personality.

● Preheat the oven to 350°F (180°C). Prepare a 6-cup standard (½-cup/125-ml) muffin pan by greasing or inserting liners.

● In a large mixing bowl, mix together the flour and sugar. In a small mixing bowl, combine the egg, milk, 1 oz (30 g) of the melted butter, and all but ½ tablespoon of the passion fruit pulp. Add all at once to the flour mixture and stir just until moistened. Divide evenly among the prepared cups.

● Bake until the tops spring back when lightly tapped, 20–25 minutes. Cool on a wire rack in the pan for 5 minutes, then turn out to cool completely.

● For the icing, sift the confectioners' (icing) sugar into a small bowl. Add the remaining melted butter and enough of the remaining passion fruit pulp to give the icing a smooth, spreadable consistency. Spread the icing over the cooled cupcakes and allow it to set before serving.

Make It Different!

● *Although passion fruit seeds are edible, you can strain them out of the pulp if you prefer.*

● *Substitute puréed ripe mango pulp for the passion fruit in the batter and icing.*

● *Add an extra tropical touch by topping the icing with bits of candied (glacé) pineapple.*

makes 6

1 cup (5 oz/155 g)
self-rising flour

⅓ cup (2¾ oz/80 g)
superfine (castor) sugar

1 egg, lightly beaten

¼ cup (2 fl oz/60 ml) milk

1⅓ oz (40 g) butter, melted

¼ cup (2 fl oz/60 ml) plus
1½ tablespoons passion
fruit pulp including seeds
(about 3 ripe passion fruit)

½ cup (2½ oz/75 g)
confectioners' (icing) sugar

makes 6

2 tablespoons butter

3 tablespoons honey

1 cup (5 oz/155 g)
self-rising flour

¼ teaspoon baking powder

½ teaspoon ground
cinnamon

½ teaspoon ground ginger

½ teaspoon ground
cardamom

¾ cup (4 oz/125 g) plus
2 tablespoons slivered
almonds

1 egg, lightly beaten

⅓ cup (3 fl oz/90 ml) milk

6 sugar cubes, roughly
crushed

honey & spice
cupcakes

Almonds and sugar cubes make a crunchy topping for adult cupcakes that children will like, too.

● Preheat the oven to 350°F (180°C). Prepare a 6-cup standard (½-cup/125-ml) muffin pan by greasing or inserting liners.

● In a small saucepan, melt the butter and honey together over low heat. Set aside to cool. In a large mixing bowl, whisk together the flour, baking powder, and spices. Set aside. In a food processor, finely grind a scant ½ cup (2 oz/60 g) of the almonds. Stir them into the dry ingredients and make a well in the center. In a small mixing bowl, combine the egg, milk, and butter-honey mixture. Add all at once to the dry ingredients and stir just until moistened. Divide the batter evenly among the prepared cups. Sprinkle the tops with the remaining almonds and the sugar cubes, lightly pressing down.

● Bake until the tops spring back when lightly tapped, 20–25 minutes. Cool in the pan on a wire rack for 5 minutes. Serve warm, or turn out onto the rack to cool completely.

Make It Different!

● *Substitute coarsely chopped hazelnuts (filberts) for the almonds in the batter and topping.*

● *Use crushed brown sugar cubes in place of the white sugar cubes.*

● *Drizzle the warm cupcakes with the caramel sauce from the recipe for Warm Date-Nut Cupcakes (page 43).*

chocolate & candied ginger cupcakes

Candied ginger and walnuts bring the flavor of a sophisticated confection to these easy cupcakes.

- Preheat the oven to 350°F (180°C). Prepare a 6-cup standard (½-cup/125-ml) muffin pan by greasing or inserting liners.

- In the top pan of a double boiler, combine 1 tablespoon of the cream with the chocolate and stir over (not touching) simmering water until combined. Stir in 3 tablespoons of the butter and set aside to cool. In a mixing bowl, using an electric mixer on medium-high speed, beat the egg and sugar until pale. Stir into the chocolate mixture alternately with the flour, baking soda, two thirds of the ginger, and the walnuts.

- Divide the batter evenly among the prepared cups. Bake until the tops spring back when lightly tapped, 20–25 minutes. Cool in the pan on a wire rack for 5 minutes, then turn out and cool completely.

- For the icing, in a small saucepan combine the remaining ginger, 2 tablespoons of the remaining cream, and the brown sugar. Bring to a boil, stirring frequently, then reduce the heat and simmer for 10 minutes. Remove from the heat and whisk in the remaining butter. Refrigerate for 10 minutes. With an electric mixer on medium-high speed, beat the remaining cream until soft peaks form. Gently fold into the cooled mixture. Spread or pipe over the cupcakes.

Make It Different!

- *Use pecans in place of the walnuts.*

- *Decorate the frosting with extra candied (glacé) ginger and cocoa powder.*

- *Substitute Vanilla Buttercream (page 15) for the frosting in the recipe.*

makes 6

½ cup (4 fl oz/125 ml)
heavy (double) cream

3 oz (90 g) plus
1 tablespoon semisweet
(plain) chocolate chips

¼ cup (2 oz/60 g) butter

1 egg

⅓ cup (3 oz/90 g) plus
1 tablespoon sugar

1 cup (5 oz/155 g)
self-rising flour, sifted

¼ teaspoon baking soda
(bicarbonate of soda)

2 oz (60 g) candied
(glacé) ginger, chopped

⅓ cup (1½ oz/45 g)
plus 1 tablespoon
chopped walnuts

¼ cup (1½ oz/45 g)
firmly packed brown sugar

makes 6

1 egg

1 tablespoon plus 1 teaspoon sugar

¼ cup (1⅓ oz/40 g) all-purpose (plain) flour

¼ teaspoon baking powder

2 tablespoons flaked (dessicated) coconut

1 tablespoon butter, melted

2 tablespoons raspberry jam

Confectioners' (icing) sugar, for dusting

coconut & raspberry
cupcakes

Hidden in its center, each of these little gems contains a delicious spoonful of raspberry jam.

● In a mixing bowl, using a hand-held electric mixer on medium-high speed, beat the egg and sugar until the mixture is thick and pale and forms a ribbon when the beaters are lifted out. In a separate bowl, whisk together the flour and baking powder. With a rubber spatula, fold about half of the flour mixture into the egg mixture; then fold in half of the coconut; and, finally, repeat with the remainder of each. Fold in the melted butter. Cover the bowl and chill in the refrigerator for 25 minutes.

● Meanwhile, preheat the oven to 400°F (200°C). Prepare a 6-cup standard (½-cup/125-ml) muffin pan by greasing or inserting liners.

● Distribute half of the batter evenly among the prepared cups. Spoon 1 scant teaspoon of jam into the center of each cup. Cover with the remaining batter. Bake until the tops spring back when lightly tapped, 15–20 minutes. Turn out onto wire racks to cool completely.

● Before serving, dust the cupcakes with confectioner's (icing) sugar.

> ### Make It Different!
>
> ● *Try other flavors of jam, such as strawberry, blueberry, apricot, or your favorite marmalade.*
>
> ● *In place of jam, try bottled lemon curd.*
>
> ● *Instead of dusting sugar on top, try Vanilla Buttercream (page 15) or the glaze from the Poundcake Cupcakes recipe (page 16).*

chocolate truffle
cupcakes

These rich little cakes contain a double dose of chocolate, making them as rich and sweet as the candies for which they are named.

● Preheat the oven to 400°F (200°C). Prepare a 6-cup standard (½-cup/125-ml) muffin pan by greasing or inserting liners.

● In a mixing bowl, use a hand-held electric mixer on medium-high speed to beat the butter and sugar together until light and fluffy. Add the egg and beat well. In another bowl, whisk together the flour, cocoa powder, and baking powder. In alternate batches, stir the melted chocolate, dry ingredients, and milk into the butter mixture. Distribute the batter among the prepared cups.

● Bake until the tops spring back when lightly tapped, about 20 minutes. Cool in the pan for 5 minutes, then turn out onto a wire rack to cool completely. Serve warm or cool, topped with the chocolate glaze and candies.

Make It Different!

● *For extra-decadent results, embed a small chocolate truffle candy in the center of the batter in each cup before baking.*

● *Top the cupcakes with Cream Cheese Frosting (page 24).*

● *Instead of the glaze, simply dust the cupcakes with confectioners' (icing) sugar.*

makes 6

¼ cup (2 oz/60 g) butter

3 oz (90 g) sugar

1 egg

1 cup (5 oz/155 g) self-rising flour

1 tablespoon unsweetened cocoa powder

½ teaspoon baking powder

3⅓ oz (100 g) bittersweet (dark) chocolate, melted

½ cup (4 fl oz/125 ml) milk

2 batches Chocolate Glaze (page 59)

Chocolate candies, for decoration

makes 6

⅔ cup (3½ oz/105 g) all-purpose (plain) flour

1½ teaspoons baking powder

¼ teaspoon ground cinnamon

Pinch of baking soda (bicarbonate of soda)

1 tablespoon plus 2 teaspoons firmly packed light brown sugar

3 tablespoons cream cheese

1 egg, lightly beaten

¼ cup (2 fl oz/60 ml) milk

1½ tablespoons butter, melted

¼ teaspoon vanilla extract (essence)

⅓ cup (1½ oz/45 g) raspberries

Confectioners' (icing) sugar, for serving

raspberry cream
cupcakes

The perfect elegant yet easy ending for a party, this recipe works well with fresh or frozen berries.

• Preheat the oven to 350°F (180°C). Prepare a 6-cup standard (½-cup/125-ml) muffin pan by greasing or inserting liners.

• In a mixing bowl, whisk together the flour, baking powder, cinnamon, and baking soda. Stir in the brown sugar. Using a pastry blender, cut in the cream cheese until the mixture resembles pea-sized crumbs. In a small bowl, combine the egg, milk, melted butter, and vanilla. Add all at once to the flour mixture and stir just until moistened. Fold in the berries. Divide the mixture evenly among the prepared cups.

• Bake until the tops spring back when lightly tapped, 20–25 minutes. Cool in the pan on a wire rack for 10 minutes, then turn out and cool completely. Before serving, dust lightly with confectioners' sugar.

Make It Different!

• *Substitute fresh or frozen blackberries or boysenberries for the raspberries.*

• *Top with a white chocolate frosting, made using the Chocolate Frosting recipe (page 8).*

• *Purée a few raspberries, strain out the seeds, and combine with confectioners' sugar to make a raspberry glaze for the cupcakes.*

fruit & chocolate chip
cupcakes

Like little fruit cakes with the addition of chocolate, these treats travel well in packed lunches.

• In a mixing bowl, use a hand-held electric mixer on medium-high speed to beat the eggs and sugar until thick and pale, about 5 minutes. With a rubber spatula, fold in all of the remaining ingredients. Cover and refrigerate for 25 minutes.

• Meanwhile, preheat the oven to 400°F (200°C). Prepare a 6-cup standard (½-cup/125-ml) muffin pan by greasing or inserting liners.

• Distribute the batter evenly among the prepared cups. Bake until the tops spring back when lightly tapped, about 20 minutes. Cool in the pan for 2–3 minutes before turning out onto a wire rack to cool completely. Serve warm or cool.

Make It Different!

• *Replace the currants with dates or figs.*

• *Try adding hazelnuts (filberts), walnuts, or pecans in place of the almonds.*

• *For a traditional fruitcake flavor, add 1 teaspoon rum extract (essence) to the batter.*

makes 6

2 eggs

⅓ cup (3 oz/90 g) sugar

⅔ cup (3¼ oz/95 g) all-purpose (plain) flour

½ teaspoon baking powder

⅓ cup (3 oz/90 g) butter, melted

2½ tablespoons chopped dried apricots

1½ tablespoons finely chopped candied (glacé) cherries

½ tablespoon dried currants

½ tablespoon finely chopped blanched almonds

¼ cup (1⅓ oz/40 g) milk chocolate chips

½ tablespoon chopped candied (glacé) ginger

makes 6

cupcakes

¾ cup (4 oz/125 g) semisweet (plain) chocolate chips

6 tablespoons (90 g) unsalted butter

½ teaspoon peppermint extract (essence)

½ cup (2 oz/60 g) cake (soft-wheat) flour

2 tablespoons unsweetened cocoa powder

2 eggs, separated

½ cup (4 oz/125 g) sugar

⅛ teaspoon salt

white chocolate mint icing

2 ounces (60 g) white chocolate, chopped

1 tablespoon heavy (double) cream

½ teaspoon peppermint extract (essence)

chocolate glaze

⅔ cup (3⅓ oz/100 g) semisweet (plain) chocolate chips

2 tablespoons heavy (double) cream

6 purchased chocolate after-dinner mints, for garnish

after-dinner mint
cupcakes

These cupcakes feature the sophisticated flavors of a treat typically enjoyed with a good cup of coffee.

- Preheat the oven to 350°F (180°C). Prepare a 6-cup standard (½-cup/125-ml) muffin pan by greasing or inserting liners.

- For the cupcakes, in a small saucepan over very low heat, melt the chocolate and butter. Stir in the peppermint and set aside. In a medium bowl, whisk together the flour and cocoa. In another bowl, with an electric mixer on medium speed, beat the egg yolks and half of the sugar until pale. Stir in the chocolate. In a clean bowl, with clean beaters, beat the egg whites and salt to soft peaks. Beat in the remaining sugar until stiff peaks form. Stir the flour mixture into the chocolate mixture. With a rubber spatula, fold in the egg whites in three batches. Divide the batter among the prepared cups. Bake 20–25 minutes. Cool on a wire rack for 10 minutes, then turn out and cool completely.

- Meanwhile, make the icing. In a double boiler, melt the white chocolate and cream together. Stir in the peppermint. Cool to room temperature. Remove the cupcake liners. With a serrated knife, cut the crown from each cupcake. Spread some icing on the bottom. Replace the crown. Refrigerate 30 minutes.

- For the glaze, in a saucepan, heat the chocolate and cream over low heat until the chocolate is almost melted. Remove from the heat and stir until smooth. Cool to room temperature but still fluid. Drizzle over each cupcake. Decorate with after-dinner mints and leave until set.

Make It Different!

- *Use the Red-Hot Red Velvet Cupcakes batter (page 36), omitting the cinnamon candies.*

- *Switch the positions of the icing and glaze.*

- *Decorate with crushed candy cane pieces.*

ingredients glossary

A guide to selecting and storing the best ingredients for the recipes in this book.

bananas Use slightly overripe bananas for baking. Green or unripe ones will ripen in a few days at room temperature. Store ripe bananas in the refrigerator for several days.

berries Always look for fragrant, deeply colored, unbruised, slightly soft fruit. Refrigerate for up to a few days, unwashed and loosely covered in a single layer on a paper towel-lined tray.

cherries Look for deeply colored, plump, shiny, unblemished fruit and store the cherries covered in the refrigerator for up to 4 days.

chocolate Milk chocolate is a blend of at least 15 percent pure chocolate, extra cocoa butter, sugar, and milk solids. Semisweet (plain) contains at least 35 percent pure chocolate, extra cocoa butter, and sugar; less sweet bittersweet (dark) may be substituted. Unsweetened is pure chocolate with no sugar or flavoring. Cocoa powder is ground pure chocolate with very little cocoa butter. Well wrapped in a cool, dry place, chocolate will keep up to 4 months. (See also "White Chocolate.")

citrus The juicy flesh and the aromatic oils stored in the colored outermost layer of the peel, called the zest, of lemons, limes, and oranges add tart-sweet flavor to cupcakes. Select firm, heavy fruit with bright color; store 2 to 3 weeks in the refrigerator.

coconut Rich and exotic, the dried meat of the coconut is widely available in a number of forms, including longer shredded pieces and smaller flaked bits, either sweetened or unsweetened. Coconut will keep for months if stored airtight.

cooking fats Butter and margarine make cupcakes rich and tender. Use stick or block forms, not whipped. Both keep for 1 month, well wrapped in the refrigerator, or 6 months in the freezer.

dried fruit Dried fruit, including dates, apricots, cherries, and cranberries, are favorite and wholesome additions to cupcakes. Unopened packages of dried fruit will stay in good condition almost indefinitely. Once opened, transfer to a plastic bag and refrigerate. (See also "Raisins.")

eggs Cupcakes gain rich flavor, tenderness, and fluffiness from eggs. Shell color, brown or white, makes no difference. Refrigerate in the carton for up to 5 weeks.

flour Wheat flour gives muffins their structure and crumb. All-purpose (plain) flour has a medium protein content suitable for most baking, while cake (soft-wheat) flour is lower in protein for a finer crumb. Whole-wheat flour is coarsely milled from the entire kernel. Store white flour in an airtight container in the pantry for 10 to 15 months, whole-wheat for up to 5 months.

ginger The underground stem of a semitropical plant, ginger is marketed fresh, dried, ground into a powder, and as crystallized or "candied" pieces. Select fresh ginger that is firm, not shriveled; wrap in a paper towel and refrigerate for 2 to 3 weeks. Store ground and crystallized ginger in an airtight container for up to 6 months.

leaveners Chemical leavening agents help cupcakes rise. Baking powder reacts with liquid and/or heat to produce carbon dioxide bubbles that cause batters to expand. Baking soda (bicarbonate of soda), when exposed to moisture and an acidic ingredient like buttermilk, yogurt, chocolate, or lemon juice, also releases carbon dioxide. Replace both every 3 months.

nuts All nuts add richness, flavor, and crunch. You'll find them in supermarkets packaged and in bulk in a number of forms. Store airtight in the refrigerator or freezer.

ingredients glossary

raisins (sultanas) Dark seedless raisins, or sultanas, have deep color and flavor, while golden seedless are pale and tangy; both are interchangeable in recipes, though the term "raisins" generally refers just to the dark form of dried grapes. Store unopened packages in a dry place; once opened, seal and refrigerate or freeze.

spices Ground dried sweet spices like cinnamon, cloves, allspice, nutmeg, and ginger add distinctive character to cupcakes. All are available ground in the market's seasonings aisle. Buy in small quantities, as they lose flavor after about 6 months. Store in a cool, dark, dry place.

sugars Dark brown sugar combines granulated (white) sugar and molasses for a deep, rich flavor. Light brown sugar has less molasses and a lighter taste. Typically used for frostings and icings, powdered sugar, also called confectioners' or icing sugar, is ground and mixed with a small amount of cornstarch to prevent caking. Granulated (white) sugar is available in fine white crystals (most common) and superfine (castor). Store sugars indefinitely in airtight containers.

sweeteners, liquid Made by bees from floral nectar, honey is sweet and sticky and imparts rich flavor and perfume. Molasses, a byproduct of sugar-cane refining, comes in two interchangeable forms: sweet and mild light molasses and more full-bodied, less sweet dark molasses. Unopened bottles will last up to a year in a cool spot; after opening, store as directed on the label.

white chocolate Although not a true chocolate, because it lacks the pure chocolate solids that make that ingredient brown, white chocolate does contain cocoa butter along with sugar, dry milk solids, and other flavors. Store in a cool, dry place.

index

Honey & spice cupcakes 47
    Icing
        chocolate icing 28
        white chocolate mint icing 59
        white icing 28
        See also Frosting, Glaze

    Lemon
        lemon coconut cupcakes 27
        poundcake cupcakes with
          lemon-lime glaze 16
    Lime
        poundcake cupcakes with
          lemon-lime glaze 16

Mexican chocolate streusel cupcakes 39
Mint, after-dinner cupcakes 59
Molasses
    gingerbread pear cupcakes 23

Nutmeg
    double-decker carrot cupcakes 24
Nuts
    chocolate & candied ginger cupcakes 48
    chocolate cherry cupcakes 32
    double-decker carrot cupcakes 24
    fruit & chocolate chip cupcakes 56
    honey & spice cupcakes 47
    peanut butter & banana cupcakes 12
    pecan coffeecake cupcakes 19
    warm date-nut cupcakes with
      caramel sauce 43

Orange zest cupcakes 20

Passion fruit cupcakes 44
Peanut butter & banana cupcakes 12
Pear, gingerbread cupcakes 23

Pecans
    pecan coffeecake cupcakes 19
    warm date-nut cupcakes
      with caramel sauce 43
Pineapple upside-down cupcakes 35
Poundcake cupcakes with
    lemon-lime glaze 16

Raspberries
    coconut & raspberry cupcakes 51
    raspberry cream cupcakes 55
    white chocolate raspberry cupcakes 40
Red-hot red velvet cupcakes 36

Sour cream
    Mexican chocolate streusel
      cupcakes 39
    pecan coffeecake cupcakes 19
    poundcake cupcakes with
      lemon-lime glaze 16
    vanilla sour cream cupcakes 11

Vanilla
    pecan coffeecake cupcakes 19
    poundcake cupcakes with
      lemon-lime glaze 16
    vanilla buttercream 15
    vanilla rainbow cupcakes 15
    vanilla sour cream cupcakes 11
    white icing 28

Walnuts
    chocolate & candied ginger
      cupcakes 48
    double-decker carrot cupcakes 24
Warm date-nut cupcakes with
    caramel sauce 43
White chocolate
    white chocolate mint icing 59
    white chocolate raspberry cupcakes 40